A Teen's Guide to Peer Pressure

A Teen's Guide to Peer Pressure

Freedom from Worrying About What Others Think

Paul David Tripp

New Growth Press
newgrowthpress.com

New Growth Press, Greensboro, NC 27401
newgrowthpress.com

Cover Design: Dan Stelzer
Interior Typesetting and Ebook: Lisa Parnell,
lparnellbookservices.com

ISBN: 978-1-64507-643-8 (print)
ISBN: 978-1-64507-644-5 (ebook)

Library of Congress Cataloging-in-Publication Data on file

Printed in India

30 29 28 27 26 1 2 3 4 5

I will never forget my first day of high school. I was moving from a small private elementary school where I knew everyone to a large public high school where I knew no one. I was terrified I wouldn't be accepted. My Christian upbringing only added to my worries. I was afraid that everyone's values would be light-years away from mine.

My mind was filled with questions fueled by my anxiety:

- Would I be liked?
- Would I be accepted?
- Would I be considered "cool"?
- What group would I fit in with?
- How much rejection and mockery would I have to endure before I was finally "in"?

That first day of high school I felt like an alien from another planet. I knew it wasn't true, but I felt like every eye in the entire place was sizing me up.

What was the source of my fear, stress, and anxiety? Peer pressure. When we talk about *peer pressure*, you may think it only has to do with feeling pressure from your friends to be like them or to do what they are doing. But peer pressure is actually a much bigger issue. It's fear of people and making what others think (or might think) about you the most important thing in life.

What are some signs that peer pressure is affecting your life?

Red Flags That Peer Pressure May Be Affecting You (Check all that apply.)

- ☐ Anxiety before being in settings with your peers (party, camp, youth group, school, etc.).
- ☐ Fear of missing out—constantly wondering what others are thinking/saying/doing.
- ☐ Tracking your friends' (and others') activities on social media—wondering why you weren't included or feeling rejected if you weren't invited.
- ☐ Spending time thinking about how to be accepted by those you want to like you.
- ☐ OR feeling rejected by others and determining to stay away from anyone who might reject you.

- ☐ Going over and over something you said in a group and wondering how it was received.
- ☐ Doing things you don't think are right to become part of a group (for example—talking about others, taking risks, trying alcohol and drugs).
- ☐ Anger when anyone (like your parents or other adults) tries to talk to you about your friend group.
- ☐ Lack of interest in spiritual things. Your friends (or those you want to be friends with) are more important to you than a relationship with God.

How many of the boxes did you check? Checking any one of them can be a sign that peer pressure is affecting your thoughts, mood, and actions. As human beings, this is natural. I wish I could say that peer pressure no longer affects me, but I still worry about what others think! Yet I trust in Jesus, knowing that his Spirit is working to change me and free me from my bondage to the opinions of others.

When you think about it, the ways people deal with the pressure to be accepted causes a lot of stress! And this kind of stress doesn't go away as you get older. The way you handle peer pressure now will impact the rest of your life. So now is a good time to start learning how to live freely and confidently no matter what the people around you are doing and saying.

This is a learning process—and you will be in it for a lifetime, but it starts with getting God's wisdom on this issue. God, who made you and knows you better than anyone else, says many useful and lifegiving things in his Word—the Bible—about peer pressure that will keep you steady through any relational drama.

What Does God Say About Peer Pressure?

Peer pressure is not just an issue for teenagers—it's a human issue. The Bible calls peer pressure "fear of man," and we all struggle with it. Each of us has given the people around us more power than God intended them to have. We all can be fearful about what people think of us, how they will respond to us, or what they may do to us. We all have people in our lives whose opinion means more to us than it should or who have the power to control us more than they should. God knows we have this struggle, so he talks about it in the Bible:

> If you are afraid of people, it will trap you.
> But if you trust in the LORD, he will
> keep you safe. (Proverbs 29:25 NIrV)

> Do not put your trust in princes,
> in human beings, who cannot save.
> When their spirit departs, they return
> to the ground;
> on that very day their plans come to
> nothing. (Psalm 146:3–4)

Notice that God is speaking to everyone in these verses. He is calling everyone (not just teenagers) to trust in the eternal God who saves them, instead of people who cannot save and will soon die. You are dealing with the same universal human struggle everyone deals with—putting your trust in the wrong thing.

The Root of the Problem

This might sound strange, but even though it seems like your problem comes from how you relate to those around you, the Bible is very clear that the reason the opinions of people control you more than they should is rooted in our relationship with God. How you live in a "vertical" relationship with God will impact the way you interact in "horizontal" relationships with other people.

The apostle Paul explains it by saying everyone has "exchanged the truth about God for a lie, and worshiped and served created things rather than the Creator" (Romans 1:25). We naturally exchange worship and service of the Creator for worship and service of the creation. What does that have to do with the pressure you feel to be accepted and loved by your peers? The reason you are filled with anxiety, fear rejection, and obsess over your relationships is because you have put the people around you in the place of God.

So the identity, meaning, purpose, security, motivation, and sense of well-being you are meant to get from God, you try to get from the people around you.

The result?

You become focused on how those people are responding to you, controlled by what they think of you, and fearful of what they might do to you.

You Are in a Vulnerable Time of Life

Although everyone struggles with others' opinions of them and their relationships, during the teenage years, you are especially susceptible to struggling in this area. Why? Because you are building an independent network of relationships. Your parents are no longer in charge of your friendships and relationships. No one is setting up "play dates" for you any longer. Instead, you are starting to build relationships on your own.

So how others respond to you now takes on new importance. You are also beginning to establish a sense of identity and belonging that is separate from your family. You are trying to work out where you fit in and where you belong and who you belong with. Along with those questions comes an awareness of how others are defining you and who is accepting or rejecting you.

All of these new challenges can also bring new fears. What God calls "fear of people" can be expressed in deep (and sometimes paralyzing) relational fears. What are some of those fears?

- ***Fear of being known*** for who you really are.
    - ***Result:*** Trying to become the person you think your peers want you to be.
- ***Fear of rejection.***
    - ***Result:*** Become skilled at doing and saying things that you hope will bring you acceptance with certain people or groups.
- ***Fear of hurt*** and mistreatment.
    - ***Result:*** Watching out for and trying to avoid situations that seem relationally dangerous or painful.

Notice that the result of acting on these fears is that you can't be yourself, you can't disclose to others who you really are, and you are not free to move toward others in a real way. Fear of people keeps you from growing and being your authentic self that is known and loved by those around you. How can others care for you when they don't even know the real you?

Replacing Fear of People with Fear of God—the Only Lasting Solution

Attaching your identity, meaning, and purpose to the acceptance of another human being will only increase your fears. Building your life on others' opinions is an alienating and unsteady foundation. But there is hope! You can turn to God and fear him.

Psalm 34:9 gets right to the heart of the matter: "Fear the Lord, you his holy people, for those who fear him lack nothing."

Fearing God isn't like fearing people. What does it mean to fear the Lord? It means God is your ultimate treasure, your biggest motivator, and the person you live for. Fearing God means putting him first in your life and making his never-failing love your sure foundation.

Fearing God means living every day in awe of his power and grateful for his grace. It means wanting to please God by what you think, desire, say, and do. And it means finding fulfillment in pleasing him and being a part of what he is doing on earth. Only when you find your identity, meaning, and purpose in the Lord will you be able to stop trying to get those things from your peers.

When anyone, at any age, begins living to please God instead of people, it brings a radical transformation. God can do this in you. I have watched young people learn to put God first in their lives and their hearts and that changed their deepest desires and motivations.

How Can You Grow in Putting God First?

As you read, you might be wishing that you could be free of being afraid of other people and hoping that you could be real with everyone you talk to. But how does that happen? Jesus says this about where our words and actions come from:

> "But the things that come out of a person's mouth come from the heart, and these defile them. For out of the heart come evil thoughts—murder, adultery, sexual immorality, theft, false testimony, slander." (Matthew 15:18–19)

Jesus is pointing out that everything we say and do comes from what we want the most—deep inside of us. If your deepest desire is to be accepted by the people around you, you will do and say things to try and make that happen.

Who Can Change What You Want the Most?

You probably already know the "Sunday school answer" to that question is that only God can change you. But take some time to think a bit more deeply about how you are living and what your relationships are like. Would you like to be free from worrying about others' opinions and whether or not you are accepted by others? Would you like to live an authentic life where you trust God for all the hard parts of your relationships? If the answer is yes, then change can begin as you admit to God that you cannot free yourself and cry out for his help. What should you ask for?

1. ***Faith.*** Up to now perhaps you have put your faith in yourself and your own ability to get what you want from life and from your friends. But now you realize that the result is fear, anxiety, and never being able to rest. Jesus says that he is standing at the door of your heart and knocking (Revelation 3:20). He wants to come in and be with you. Turn to him and he will turn your world right side up. Listen to this invitation from Jesus: "Come to me, all you who are weary and burdened, and I will give you rest" (Matthew 11:28). Would you like some rest from all the worry and anxiety that comes from caring more about people's opinion than God's? Jesus invites you to rest in him.
2. ***Forgiveness.*** Along with turning to Jesus in faith comes the gift of forgiveness. When you put people and your

desire to be accepted by them before your love for God—that's going your own way and that's what God calls sin (Isaiah 53:6). Jesus gave his life so that all who come to him and ask are forgiven. His death paid for all your sins. You don't have to be afraid to admit you are wrong anymore (1 John 1:8–9). Asking God to forgive you and change you will fill you with his power, his love, and his presence. Those are the things that will give you true peace.

3. ***New identity.*** When you turn to Jesus in faith and ask for forgiveness, you have a whole new identity—a child of God with Jesus as your brother. You have joined the best group in the world! You are accepted by God. Jesus is your friend. He will never turn his back on you. He will never leave you out or reject you. You are a child of the powerful and loving God of the universe. Everything he has is yours. Seeking to base your identity in the crowd you hang around with will leave you

frustrated and empty. But relying on Jesus will fill you with peace.

4. ***Prayer.*** Now you can talk over all your problems and desires with your best friend, Jesus. What do you need from God? Tell him all about it. What do you wish he would change? Ask him for help from above. And pray for your own heart. Pray that you will put Jesus first and be released from your fear of others.
5. ***Self-understanding.*** Ask God to help you understand yourself and why you do what you do. Take some time to think about your relationships. Ask God to show you why you are hanging out with certain friends. Are you looking for acceptance? Belonging? There is nothing wrong with that—but when it overtakes our love for God, then we are asking for our friendships to do what only God can do for us. Ask God to give you his perspective on your friendships. One thing to be alert for is that because we are sinners, we all have a

strange attraction to things that are outside of God's fences. The forbidden cookie seems more attractive and delicious. We have a dangerous curiosity about dangerous things. All of us are rebellious in some way, and all of us can be attracted to others who are also rebelling. Ask God to search your heart to show you if you are being tempted by the attractiveness of things outside of God's good boundaries for us.

Jesus said that you know a tree by its fruit (Matthew 7:15–20). An apple tree produces apples because it is an apple tree right down to its roots. If it had peach roots, it couldn't produce apples. In the same way, when your heart is changed by Jesus, the roots of love for God will produce the fruit of love for others. This is the way of rest and peace—not in trying to please others or getting their approval and acceptance, but in loving God and loving others. This is what you were made for, and it's the way to rich relationships that encourage you and others. You can't do this on your own, but God can do this in you. Look to Jesus—the only person who can bring lasting change and give you true soul rest.

MORE FROM PAUL DAVID TRIPP

A QUEST FOR MORE

Paul David Tripp

Chasing popularity, success, or approval can feel empty fast. In this challenging book, Paul David Tripp calls you to live for something bigger than yourself—God's kingdom. Learn how to let go of small, self-focused goals and grow into a Christ-centered life filled with purpose, freedom, and lasting impact.

HOW PEOPLE CHANGE

Paul David Tripp

Ever feel stuck in the same habits, no matter how hard you try to change? How People Change shows how real, lasting change starts in your heart—not just your behavior. Using a clear, biblical model, this book helps you understand how God is at work in you and gives real hope for growing and changing through Christ.

RELATIONSHIPS: A MESS WORTH MAKING

Paul David Tripp

Friendships, family, and dating can get messy fast. Relationships: A Mess Worth Making shows why relationships are hard—and why they're worth it. With real-life stories and gospel-centered wisdom, this book helps you handle conflict, communicate better, and grow through relationships instead of giving up on them.

MORE FROM OUR TEEN MINIBOOK SERIES

A TEEN'S GUIDE TO ANXIETY

Eliza Huie

School stress, sports pressure, and social anxiety can feel overwhelming. Counselor Eliza Huie helps you recognize anxiety, talk with a trusted adult, and use the simple N-E-A-R steps to calm your mind and body. You're not weak, and you're not alone. When everything feels overwhelming, God is near and ready to help.

A TEEN'S GUIDE TO EATING DISORDERS

Lainey Greer

Social media and constant comparison can twist how you see food, your body, and yourself. In this honest minibook, Lainey Greer shares her story, explains warning signs of eating disorders, and reminds you that you matter. God sees you fully and offers real hope, healing, and support.

NEW GROWTH PRESS newgrowthpress.com